Praising
the God
of Grace

Praising the God of Grace

The Theology of Charles Wesley's Hymns

Leader

JOHN P. GILBERT

Abingdon Press
Nashville

PRAISING THE GOD OF GRACE
THE THEOLOGY OF CHARLES WESLEY'S HYMNS

The Library of Congress has cataloged the leader's guide as follows:

Yrigoyen, Charles, 1937–
   Praising the God of grace : the theology of Charles Wesley's hymns / Charles Yrigoyen, Jr.
   p. cm.
   Includes bibliographical references.
   ISBN-0-687-03668-2
   1. Wesley, Charles, 1707-1788. 2. United Methodist Church
   (U.S.)—Hymns—History and criticism. 3. Hymns, English—History and criticism. I. Title.

BV415.A1Y75 2005
264'.23'092—dc22

                                                                2004024180

05 06 07 08 09 10 11 12 13 14—10 9 8 7 6 5 4 3 2 1
MANUFACTURED IN THE UNITED STATES OF AMERICA

Contents

Introduction

Y ou are about to embark on an exciting journey, a journey into the roots of our faith as Christians.

Some of those roots go back to the time before Abraham and before the nations of Judah and Israel. Many of those roots go back to the life, death, and resurrection of Jesus Christ and our recognition of him as our Lord and Savior. And some of those roots go back to two fascinating figures who lived in eighteenth-century England, brothers by the names of John and Charles Wesley.

The two Wesleys are usually credited with beginning the movement that became the Wesleyan or Methodist revival, a spiritual awakening in England and North America. That revival led to the creation of a family of denominations now known as Wesleyan.

One of the Wesley brothers, Charles, was a gifted poet and musician. He simply could not help singing his joy in the Lord, proclaiming his faith in song, and putting his witness to music. Consequently, those denominations that trace their roots to the Wesleys are "singing churches." The members of these congregations love to proclaim their faith in Christ Jesus through music.

Was Charles Wesley wise enough to know that the words of hymns are easier to memorize than passages of prose? Did he know that people would "absorb" a great deal of theology just by singing joyfully the hymns he wrote? We cannot say for sure. We can say that the faith and theology of the churches that trace their lineage to the Wesleys are proclaimed mightily through song and that many members of the churches "know what they believe" through the words of the hymns they sing each Sunday.

In this eight-session study of the book *Praising the God of Grace* by Charles Yrigoyen Jr., you will be looking at many of the basic beliefs and understandings of the denominations that trace their history to the hymns Charles Wesley wrote for "the Methodist societies" to sing. We will discover the messages he wanted to communicate through the words of hymns, and we will recognize the beliefs we share as a result of singing those hymns over and over again. One word of caution: This is a limited study. We cannot probe all the details of Wesleyan theology, faith, and belief in eight sessions. In short, we hope that this study will whet your appetite to delve more deeply into the hymns of the Wesleyan revival, both those of Charles Wesley and those added to the hymnals of the Wesleyan family of churches over the years.

Suggestions for Organizing and Conducting Group Sessions

Keep your study group small—about twelve to sixteen persons is a good number. This is not a lecture or presentation class, but a discussion and interaction group. If more than sixteen persons show interest in studying this material, form two groups.

Arrange your meeting space so that everyone can see everyone else face-to-face. You are going to be talking to and with one another, not sitting passively. As leader, you should be part of the group. Do not hide behind a lectern. Join the group as one of the learners, for that is exactly what you are. (Perhaps the ideal setting is seated around tables so that group members have a place to spread their Bibles, hymnals, and notes.) Use moveable chairs if possible, for many of the learning activities described in this leader's guide suggest conversations in pairs, in threes, and in fours.

Remind your group members to bring Bibles, pencils or pens, and note paper to each session. You will also want to have copies of several different hymnals available; many of Charles Wesley's hymns are sung to a variety of tunes. Be sure to use the compact disc contained in this leader's guide. This disc provides the musical accompaniment for the theme hymns discussed in the study book, using the tunes most often associated with these hymns. Alternative tunes are also included for several of the theme hymns.

Encourage the group members to read the assigned chapters of the study book and portions of the appendix before each session. This will enrich the discussions at group sessions and augment learning on the part of all. Also, ask the group members to look up the biblical references cited in the study book chapters. The scriptures form the basis of many of Charles Wesley's hymns, and reading and rereading those Scriptures will illuminate the hymns and the faith statements they contain.

Read the words of the hymns as well as sing them. Read them aloud yourself; ask the group members to read them aloud; or read them aloud as a whole group. The focus in this study is on the words, not on the tunes. Pay careful attention to punctuation in the texts of the hymns as you read them aloud. Read the words as you would read a Scripture passage aloud; that is, with appropriate inflection, pauses at commas and periods, and so forth. Do not let the rhyming schemes detract you from the meaning of the words.

Each session plan contains the following sections: Purpose, Materials, Prepare to Teach, Begin the Session, Develop the Ideas, Draw the Session to a Close, and Optional Method. You will need to make decisions about which learning activities will be appropriate for your group and can be completed in the available length of time.

Session 1

Praising the God of Grace

Purpose

To introduce hymn writer and theologian Charles Wesley, and to discover, as Charles Wesley did, that the grace of God is operative within our lives even though we continue in sin.

Materials

A variety of hymnals, including several that contain many of Charles Wesley's hymns. Check the indices of authors and composers in the hymnals. If you have access to several copies of the same hymnal, obtain a copy for each group member. If you borrow hymnals from your sanctuary, return them before your next service of worship.

A copy of the study book for each group member.

A chalkboard, whiteboard, or large pad of paper and easel.

Paper and pencils for group members. Encourage group members to bring their own for note-taking at each session.

A Bible for each person. Choose varying translations in order to gain new insights into the meaning of passages of Scripture.

Copies of the closing prayer for each group member.

Prepare to Teach

You will want to read the entire study book as your initial preparation for leading a group. If you have questions about the life of Charles Wesley, ask your pastor for books on church history or look up *Charles Wesley* in the card catalog of your library or on the Internet.

Group members should have read chapter 1, "Praising the God of Grace," and the introduction and "England, Epworth Rectory, and Childhood" from the appendix of the study book (pp. 85-88) prior to this session. If this has not been possible, you may need to adapt some of these learning activities to allow time for group members to read from the chapter.

Mount a large piece of paper on a wall or easel in your meeting room. Construct a chronology or timeline of the life of Charles Wesley. Add to this timeline during each session as new information about Wesley is discussed by the group members. Alongside the dates of incidents in the life of Charles Wesley, jot down important dates in the history of the American colonies and the United States if possible. Be sure your group members see that the American Revolution took place late in Charles Wesley's life, but that the faith and theology exemplified by the Wesley brothers had already taken root in the colonies.

Begin the Session

Open the session with prayer, inviting God's Spirit to be powerfully present as your group discusses God's infinite love.

If group members do not know one another, you might take time for quick introductions. Ask each person to introduce herself or himself to the group and to say in a sentence or two why she or he is interested in this topic. As you introduce yourself, you might quickly remind your group members that although this study is about hymns, no one is going to have to sing a solo or even to sing as part of the group unless she or he chooses to do so.

Write these words on the chalkboard or a large piece of paper: *grace, sin, assurance.* Ask each group member to jot down a one-sentence definition of each of these words. Direct the group members to put the definitions aside; you will be coming back to them later in the session.

Develop the Ideas

Read (do not sing!) aloud the seven verses of "O For a Thousand Tongues to Sing" (pp. 1-2 in the study book) as the group members follow along. Remind the group members that this Charles Wesley hymn is about grace, but that the word *grace* occurs only once as a noun and once as an adjective *(gracious)* in these seven stanzas. Ask: What does this hymn have to say about grace? Help the group members recognize that this hymn describes the *functions* and *actions* of grace in the life of the believer.

Then, ask the group members, working in teams of three, to identify the functions of grace described in this hymn. Encourage the teams to put those functions into their own words, not simply to repeat the words of the hymn. After an appropriate length of time, call for reports from the teams in a "round-robin" fashion; that is, each team reports on one function of grace that team identified. List these functions on the chalkboard or a large piece of paper. Continue in this round-robin fashion until all of the functions named by the teams have been listed on the chalkboard or a large piece of paper.

When the functions have been identified (that is, forgiving sin, giving new life, helping the brokenhearted rejoice, and so forth), pose this question: What are some examples of grace in the Bible? Included in this list should be examples such as the creation of humankind, the mark on Cain to protect him even though he had sinned, the exodus of the Hebrews from bondage in Egypt, the gift of manna and quail in the desert as the Hebrews sought the promised land, the gift of Jesus Christ as Savior and Redeemer, the gift of the Holy Spirit, and the ultimate promises of God.

Ask: Why was God's gift of grace necessary in biblical times, and why is God's gift of grace necessary for us? Help the group members come to the understanding that the reason for God's grace is *human sinfulness.*

Next, discuss human sin. Write on the chalkboard or a large piece of paper the words *sin* and *sinful acts.* Ask persons to call out examples of each, with the goal of helping the group members realize that "sin" is the separation or estrangement from God that leads to specific sinful acts. Sin is self-centeredness and selfishness that results in actions that manifest that self-centeredness. God's grace seeks to overcome not just sinful acts but the root of those sinful acts, that is, our willful separation from God.

Continue this discussion by pointing to the Charles Wesley hymns mentioned by the writer of the study book that suggest sin is a sickness or malady. Ask the group members what this idea might mean. One crucial insight is that an illness cannot be cured by one's self; neither can we solve our own problem of sin. Ask a group member to read aloud Psalm 38:1-8 as an example of sinfulness as a profound illness. Notice, too, how Wesley referred to sin as an "infected nature," something that cannot be cleansed by a simple act of will. Wesley's use of the word *nature* also suggests that sin has taken control of our entire being, our total nature.

Remind the group members of what they read about eighteenth-century England in the appendix. Quickly list some of the kinds of sinfulness that Wesley witnessed and knew as a child and a young man. Raise this question: In what ways, if any, is our culture similar to the culture of eighteenth-century England? How is it different? (Although we no longer practice legalized slavery, ponder some of the ways in which people of today are "enslaved.") Allow a few moments for discussion, then follow with this question: If Charles Wesley perceived the sin of his day as a sickness or malady, how might the children of our day perceive the sin of our culture?

Say (preferably putting into your own words): One of the mysteries of grace is that although we willfully separate ourselves from God, God still loves us enough not only to call us back, but also to bring us back. God provides the cure for our sinfulness; God does for us what we cannot do for ourselves, even when we least deserve it. That is grace. What does grace do for us?

Form pairs or triads again, and invite each pair or triad to re-examine the list of functions of grace that your group drew out of the Wesley hymn. Then direct each pair or triad to study the section of chapter 1 titled "The Nature and Work of God's Grace" (pp. 6-10 of the study book). The writer lists four functions of God's grace; compare and contrast these four functions with the list of functions of grace that your group made.

After an appropriate length of time, hear reports from one or two of the pairs or triads. How is the group list of the functions of grace similar to and different from the four functions listed in the study book? If you could add to the list, what would you add, and why?

Have the entire group scan the section of the study book titled "Assurance and Anticipation" (pp. 10-12). Contained in the first paragraph of this section is the sentence: "This is what Wesley called assurance." Ask each person to complete this sentence stem: "For Wesley, assurance meant. . . ." Then have several persons read their completed sentences, and ask the whole group to comment (constructively!) on the sentence completions.

Ask: Why is assurance sometimes called the "forgotten component" of grace? If group members struggle a bit with responding, ask this question: How do you know that you are forgiven? How would you describe the difference in the way you felt before you were assured of forgiveness and the way you feel now? Does assurance mean that you will never sin again, that is, never become estranged from God again? Why or why not?

Have a group member read aloud 1 John 2:1-2. Ask: What does this passage say about assurance?

Draw the Session to a Close

Ask each group member to examine her or his definitions of grace, sin, and assurance written earlier in the session. Invite them to change or augment their definitions based on the conversations during the session. If some group members wish to do so, let them share the way their understanding of one or more of these words has changed.

If the group enjoys singing, invite them to sing the theme hymn for this session, "O For a Thousand Tongues to Sing," originally titled by Charles Wesley "Glory to God, and Praise and Love." Although this hymn is most often sung to the tune AZMON, it can be sung to any tune using the common meter of 86.86. For example, your group might try singing Wesley's words to the tune RICHMOND, associated with "O For a Heart to Praise My God." Both may be found on the accompanying compact disc. Oftentimes, singing a familiar hymn to a different tune yields new insights into the text of the hymn.

Close the session with this assignment: Read chapter 2 of the study book, "The Triune God" (pp. 13-23), before the next session; and consider possible answers to this question: Why does the writer deal with grace, sin, and assurance before exploring the nature of God? Also, read the section of the appendix titled "Holy Club, Reluctant Priest, and Missionary" (pp. 88-93).

End the session by inviting the group members to join in this prayer:

Lord God, I confess that I am a sinner, not just in what I do, but more in my willful separation from you. Although I cannot comprehend the expanse of the grace you shower upon me, I can and do accept that grace and commit myself ever more to believe in your love and in the ways it can transform my life. I pray in the name of the One who assures me that I am loved, Christ Jesus, my Lord. Amen.

Optional Method

The writer of the study book provides several interesting questions for discussion at the conclusion of chapter 1 (p. 00). Ask the group members to jot down responses to each of these questions. Then invite each group member to join with one other group member to share and discuss the responses. Be sure that all group members understand that they are not required to share all of their responses, only those they feel comfortable discussing with a partner.

Session 2

The Triune God

Purpose

To explore the nature of the Trinity through the use of some of the hymns of Charles Wesley; to realize that ultimately the Trinity, the source of grace, is beyond our comprehension.

Materials

See the basic list in session 1 (p. 1 of this leader's guide).

Several objects such as a candle (with a means to light it), a tea kettle with water in it, a few kernels of corn, a prism (if your meeting room is located in a sunny area), and (if you can locate one) an insect cocoon or a picture of a cocoon.

Copies of the Apostles' Creed and the Nicene Creed. You may be able to locate the creeds in the hymnals you are using during your sessions. Or talk with your pastor; almost certainly he or she will have access to these creeds in a form that can be copied for use in your session.

Prepare to Teach

Place the objects you have brought on a table so that all can see them. Before the session begins, try out the prism in your meeting room. Can you catch the sun's rays with it in such a way that the rays are divided into several different colors?

At the close of the last session, you invited group members to read chapter 2 of the study book, "The Triune God" (pp. 13-23), and the section of the appendix titled "Holy Club, Reluctant Priest, and Missionary" (pp. 88-93) before this session. Look at your time-line of Charles Wesley's life and determine what dates you will add to it during this session.

If you have newcomers in the group, you may have to adapt some of the learning activities to take into account that not all have read the assigned chapter and reading from the appendix.

Begin the Session

Open the session with a word of welcome and a prayer seeking the presence of God's Spirit with the group as you discuss the Triune God. Invite any who have joined the group since your last session to introduce themselves to the whole group. Be sure each person has access to a study book and a Bible.

Ask: What do you see in this room that might help explain the Christian concept of the Trinity? Allow a few minutes of silence as group members reflect on the question, then ask for ideas from the group. Some ideas that might be forthcoming are:

- A candle flame is somewhat like the Trinity because the candle flame is red, yellow, and blue. All of this is the candle flame, even though it appears differently.

- Water is somewhat like the Trinity in that water can be in liquid, solid (ice), or gas (steam) form. Chemically, it is still water, that is, hydrogen and oxygen combined.

- Corn is somewhat like the Trinity because it can be the corn stalk, the kernels of corn, or one of the hundreds of products made from corn. Yet it is still corn.

- The prism divides white light (from the sun) into all the colors of the spectrum. If you have access to an open window on a sunny day you can demonstrate this by allowing the sun to strike the prism and to shine through the prism onto a white surface, disclosing all the colors. Again, the point is that each of the colors is part of the light; but each of the colors is also the light.

- A cocoon is somewhat like the Trinity in that a butterfly can be in the form of a caterpillar, a cocoon, or a butterfly; but it is still the same creature.

What other analogies or metaphors might the group members offer to suggest the Trinity?

Then, ask these questions: Does any one of these analogies explain the Trinity completely? If not, why not? Help the group members understand that the Trinity remains a mystery, that is, something that we cannot comprehend completely. Like some other dimensions of life, we can experience the Trinity as we experience the Father, the Son, and the Holy Spirit; but we cannot define the Trinity precisely, nor can we explain the Trinity completely. To make this point, ask the group members what other realities might be experienced but cannot be fully defined. One classic example is love. We can and do experience love, but we cannot explain precisely why we love one person, such as a spouse, uniquely.

Develop the Ideas

Read (do not sing!) the four stanzas of "Maker [Father], in Whom We Live," the Wesley hymn that begins chapter 2 of the study book. (You might point out that the word *Father* is changed to *Maker* in some hymnals out of a concern for the use of inclusive language.)

Form four teams (a team can be as few as one person) and assign each team one of the four stanzas of this hymn. Give each team this assignment: What person of the Trinity is identified in this stanza? How do you know? What is the function or task of this person of the Trinity, as described in this stanza? That is, what does this person of the Trinity do with and for us? Locate some biblical descriptions of this person of the Trinity and be ready to share them with the whole group.

After an appropriate length of time, hear reports from each team.

Stanza one lauds God the Father. The creating God is presented perhaps most completely in the Creation stories found in the first few chapters of Genesis, Job 38–39, and Psalm 104.

Stanza two of the hymn focuses on Christ the Son who redeems humankind from bondage to sinfulness. The Gospels tell this story completely, as do the letters of Paul. The third and fourth chapters of the book of John might be cited as one example of a biblical basis for describing Christ as the Redeemer.

Stanza three of the hymn evokes the Holy Spirit's renewing power. The classic story of Pentecost, Acts 2, might be suggested as an example of this concept, although much of Jesus' statement to his disciples in John 14 could also be recalled.

Stanza four (a summary stanza) describes the entire Trinity and the love and grace that the Trinity bestows on humankind. Many of Paul's letters laud the Trinity; Romans 8:1-17 is a good example.

Ask this question for discussion by the whole group; jot group responses on a large piece of paper or the chalkboard: Why did God choose to reveal himself through the Trinity? You might amplify the question by asking this: What was God seeking to do for us in making himself available to us in Three Persons, modes, or realities? Put all the ideas offered by the group on the large piece of paper or chalkboard; do not evaluate responses until all are listed.

Seek to summarize the responses to the question by asking the following questions: At whose initiative did God appear in Three Persons? (Help the group members recognize that this was God's initiative; it was God who chose to reveal himself in Three Persons. God knew that humankind could experience the fullness of God most completely through the self-revelation in Three Persons.)

When did God choose to reveal God's self in Three Persons? (If group members are uncertain at this point, refer them to John 1:1, in which the Gospel writer declares that Christ was in the beginning with God and indeed co-creator with God. If time permits, mention that the early church struggled long and with great difficulty to understand and conclude whether the Holy Spirit was from the beginning with God and Christ or if the Holy Spirit was "created" later by God and Christ together. Some of the early church councils, such as Nicea and Constantinople in the fourth century, determined that the Holy Spirit was indeed from the beginning with God and Christ. That continues as the prevailing belief among Christians. One of the reasons for this claim is in the second Creation story, Genesis 2:7, in which the life-giving breath of God, the Spirit of God, creates humankind.)

Why did God choose to reveal himself in Three Persons? (Refer to the list of responses on the chalkboard or large piece of paper, then summarize an answer to this question in this way: God chose to reveal himself in Three Persons for our sakes and out of God's gracious love for us. God's self-revelation in Three Persons had as its purpose enabling our growing relationship with God.)

Next, explore the life of Charles Wesley for evidence of the Trinity operating in his life. Pay particular attention to the portion of the appendix in the study book assigned for this session. Ask one third of your group to look for evidence of Charles's experience of God as Creator; a second third for evidence of Charles's experience of God in Christ as the Redeemer; and the final third for examples of Charles's experience of the Holy Spirit. After an appropriate length of time, hear reports from each of the three teams. Then ask this question: Which of the Three Persons of the Trinity was most important to Charles Wesley during the formative years of college, ordination, and missionary endeavor? Encourage the group members to give reasons for their answers.

Draw the Session to a Close

One way in which Christians affirm the Triune God is through the words of the creeds. The ancient Nicene Creed displays this affirmation most prominently. Invite the group members to look at and read over the Nicene Creed. Point out how the Three Persons of the Trinity are affirmed in this creed in especially prominent ways. Note the emphasis on the creating God in the first section; on the saving God in the statements about Jesus Christ; and on the life-giving God, the Holy Spirit, in the third section of this creed. If the group members are not familiar with the Nicene Creed, you might read it aloud as a whole group. Refer also to the Apostles' Creed. Note here too the emphasis on the Three Persons of the Trinity. If the hymnal used in your church includes other affirmations of faith, invite the group to examine them for evidence of the Trinity.

If time permits and your group enjoys singing, invite the group members to sing together "Maker [Father], in Whom We Live," the hymn that begins chapter 2 in the study book. You will find the tune for this theme hymn on the compact disc included in this leader's guide.

Invite the group members to come to the next session having read chapter 3 of the study book, "Jesus, God Incarnate" (pp. 25-33), and the section of the appendix titled "Personal Pentecost, Preaching, Publishing Hymns" (pp. 93-101).

Close with this prayer:

Triune God, we thank you for revealing your most holy self in Three Persons. You have enabled us to experience you in every facet of our lives. We commit ourselves to you, Father, Son, and Holy Spirit, as you committed yourself to us through this loving self-revelation. We pray in the name of Christ Jesus. Amen.

Optional Method

This chapter on the Trinity is a difficult chapter, especially for those who have had little experience thinking theologically. The genius of Wesley's hymns is that they help make such complex concepts more manageable.

If the group is not accustomed to theological discussions, you might want to work through the study book chapter section by section, outlining each section on the chalkboard or a large piece of paper as you do so. Pause for questions and comments from the group. Although this will not be a formal lecture, it will provide a sense of guided thinking and reflection for the group members with little experience in considering theological concepts.

If you are not comfortable with leading the group through this consideration of the Trinity, you might invite your pastor or a well-qualified Sunday school teacher to do so. The use of the study book writer's questions at the end of the chapter may assist in this presentation.

Session 3

Jesus, God Incarnate

Purpose

To explore the roles of Jesus as prophet, priest, and king through the hymns of Charles Wesley and to renew our commitment to the redemption offered by and through Christ Jesus.

Materials

See the basic list in session 1 (p. 1).

Be sure each group member has a Bible. If the group members can bring various translations of the Scriptures, invite them to do so. Sharing the same passages from several different translations will enrich the group members' understandings of Jesus as truly God and truly human. Encourage them to use translations, not paraphrases. Among the best current translations are the New Revised Standard Version, the Contemporary English Version, the New International Version, and Today's English Version. Some of the group members may wish to use the King James Version. Although this is a good translation, its seventeenth-century language and grammar may make some passages difficult to comprehend.

Copies of the closing prayer for each group member.

Prepare to Teach

At the end of the second session, the group members were asked to read chapter 3 of the study book, "Jesus, God Incarnate" (pp. 25-33), and the section of the appendix titled "Personal Pentecost, Preaching, Publishing Hymns" (pp. 93-101). Be sure you have read these materials and understand them thoroughly. Examine your timeline of Charles Wesley's life, and determine what new dates and events you will add during this session.

If new members are joining your group, or if any members have not read these materials, you may need to adjust some of the learning activities.

Invite one of your group members well in advance to play the part of Charles Wesley. This person should read and study thoroughly the section "Personal Pentecost, Preaching, Publishing Hymns" in the appendix. Have this person "appear" as Charles Wesley at this meeting of your study group to tell the part of Wesley's story contained in this section in the first person. Use simple props and perhaps even a costume. Of course, your "Charles Wesley" can use notes or an outline to tell of his conversion experience, his hymn writing, his visits to prisons, and the opposition the early Methodists endured because of their unusual piety and their practice of preaching in the open air.

Begin the Session

Begin the session with a word of welcome and an opening prayer that seeks the presence of Christ among you as you study about the Incarnate God. Remind the group members of Matthew 18:20: "For where two or three are gathered in my name, I am there among them." Ask: How have you experienced the presence of Christ as you study and dialogue together?

Invite the group members to think silently for a moment, then to call out all they have learned about Jesus Christ from hymns and "church songs." Each offering should be accompanied by a fragment of the hymn or song. For example: "I know that Jesus loves me because I learned to sing: 'Jesus loves me, this I know, for the Bible tells me so.'" Or, "I am sure that Jesus arose from the dead because we sing, 'Christ the Lord is risen today!'" Jot down on the chalkboard or newsprint each idea as it is called out.

After the group members have contributed a number of characteristics or attributes of Jesus they have learned from hymns and songs, look over the list. Ask: What characteristics of Jesus are most often included in hymns? His life? His teachings? His miracles? His birth? His suffering? His resurrection? His coming again?

Probably Christians know more about Jesus' birth from hymns and songs than they know about his teachings, miracles, passion, or resurrection. Ask the group members why they think this may be so. Invite each person, working in silence, to jot down the name of her or his favorite Christmas carol, passion hymn, and resurrection hymn. Then invite each to jot down two or three other favorites that glorify Jesus Christ. If time permits at the end of the session, the group may want to sing some of the hymns listed.

Develop the Ideas

Invite three group members who read well to read aloud one stanza each of Charles Wesley's Christmas hymn, "Hark! the Herald Angels Sing." Encourage these readers to follow the punctuation carefully and to avoid "singing" the hymn. The goal here is to help the group members hear this hymn as poetry, not as a song. You might encourage the readers to imagine the hymn written in continuous lines as a narrative.

Then ask the person who read stanza one to reread it slowly as group members make note of the depictions of Jesus Christ contained in this stanza. Ask: What is the mood of this stanza; that is, is this stanza declarative? joyful? thoughtful? challenging? What makes it so? Again, try not to think of the tune to which these words are sung; instead, probe whether or not the words convey a feeling and attitude. If so, what is it?

Next, ask the group members what they learned about Jesus from this stanza, while you jot their insights on the chalkboard or a large piece of paper. For example, group members might identify Jesus as "new-born King," as "one born in Bethlehem," or as one who reconciles "God and sinners." What other characteristics did group members hear?

Ask this question for discussion by the whole group: What is meant by the line, "Joyful all ye nations rise"? Help the group members begin to understand that the Christ Child was born for all humankind, not

15

simply for the people into whose culture he was born. Then, ask: If Jesus is the new-born King, of whom is he king? Do you believe that when Charles Wesley wrote "all ye nations," he literally meant all the nations of the earth? Encourage the group members to see that Charles Wesley was proclaiming Jesus as king of all creation. If this is so, then what responsibility is placed on us as those who believe in the Christ?

Form two teams. Ask one team to read stanza two and to identify the attributes and characteristics of Jesus mentioned in the stanza. The second team should do the same for stanza three.

After an appropriate length of time, hear reports from the two teams. Invite the whole group to ask questions of clarification or amplification of the two teams.

As the team reporting on stanza two makes its report, encourage group members to look up and read John 1:1 and John 1:14. The nineteenth-century German theologian Friedrich Schleiermacher considered John 1:14 one of the most important verses in the New Testament. This verse makes the radical claim—a claim that no other religion makes—that God came to live among human beings. All other faiths report that a spokesperson, a messenger, an angel, or a prophet came to tell of their God or gods. Only Christians are sufficiently audacious to believe, on the basis of real evidence, that God, God's self, came to live among us.

If the team reporting on stanza two does not answer this question, ask: What does calling Jesus "our Emmanuel" mean? How is the word *Emmanuel* defined?

Then, turn to the report from the team considering stanza three. The study book writer quotes Philippians 2:5-8, thought by many scholars to be part of an ancient hymn. How does this passage from Philippians intersect with the words of stanza three: "Mild he lays his glory by"? What was the glory of Christ that he "laid by" or the glory of which he "emptied himself" (Philippians 2:7)?

What is the team's analysis of the three phrases that follow the word *born?* Write these on the chalkboard or a large piece of paper. Christ is "born that we no more may die." What does this phrase mean? Can you cite a biblical passage that emphasizes this concept (for example, John 11:25)? Christ is "born to raise us from the earth." What does this phrase mean? What biblical passage describes this concept (for example, John 14:1-3)? Christ is "born to give us second birth." What does this phrase mean? What biblical passage comes to mind (for example, John 3:1-16)?

Next, discuss this question as a whole group: How do the stanzas of Charles Wesley's "Hark! the Herald Angels Sing" disclose and describe Jesus Christ as prophet, that is, as one who speaks for God, proclaiming what God has given the prophet to declare? How do the stanzas describe Jesus Christ as priest? Recall in this conversation the role of the priest, especially the high priest, in the Old Testament. How do these stanzas describe Jesus Christ as king? King of what? How would you characterize and define the kingdom of Christ Jesus?

Invite your "Charles Wesley," assigned and prepared well ahead of time, to "tell his story" of conversion, of hymn writing, of social outreach, and of opposition. Encourage the group members to ask questions of "Charles Wesley," and encourage "Charles Wesley" to answer these questions to the best of his ability. If some questions remain, refer to the bibliography in the study book (pp. 109-10) for biographies of the Wesleys, in which you may be able to find answers to the inquiries.

Draw the Session to a Close

Invite the group members to sing the Charles Wesley hymn "Hark! the Herald Angels Sing" and to include the last two stanzas, found on pages 25-26 of the study book. (Recall that the music for this hymn is found on the compact disc contained in this leader's guide. Your group may sing the hymn to the music on the disc, to a piano accompaniment, or unaccompanied.)

Ask the group members to identify new insights into the nature of Jesus Christ that they gained from the last two stanzas, the ones not included in most collections of hymns and Christmas carols. Discuss as a whole group the meaning of phrases such as "Bruise in Us the Serpent's Head," "Now in Mystic Union join Thine to Ours, and Ours to Thine," and "Adam's Likeness, LORD, efface, Stamp thy Image in its Place." What does calling Jesus Christ the "Second Adam" mean?

Ask the group members to read chapter 4, "The Holy Spirit" (pp. 35-44 of the study book), and the section of the appendix titled "Marriage, Family, Controversy" (pp. 101-5) prior to the next session.

Close with this prayer, read in unison:

Lord Jesus Christ, you are all in all for each of us and for me. Although I struggle to comprehend all your incarnation means, I bow in humility before the love and grace that caused you to lay aside your divine powers and to join with us in our world. While I seek to live a life of thanksgiving in response to all you have done for me, I realize I still fall far short; and I continue to feel showered by your grace. I praise you for your love, your peace, your power, and your presence with me. Amen.

Optional Methods

"Paraphrasing" is putting into one's own words the words of Scripture, a hymn, or some other literary work.

Provide paper and pencils or pens for each group member and solid writing surfaces, if available. Explain what a "paraphrase" is, and perhaps provide a few brief examples. Emphasize that a paraphrase uses one's own words and phrases to convey the same ideas as the original writer's.

Form three teams. Ask each member of team one to paraphrase stanza one of "Hark! the Herald Angels Sing," the members of team two to paraphrase stanza two, and those in team three to paraphrase stanza three. Do not worry about rhyming or meter or about the length of the paraphrase. Simply convey the same ideas used in the stanza in the words of each member of the team.

After each person has completed a paraphrase, have the members of each team gather together and develop from their individual paraphrases a composite or team paraphrase. Encourage the teams not simply to adopt what one team member wrote as the team's work.

After an appropriate length of time, invite each team to share its paraphrased stanza with the whole group. Encourage the group members to look for new meanings and insights in the paraphrases.

If time permits, discuss some of the questions at the end of chapter 3 in the study book (p. 33).

Session 4

The Holy Spirit

Purpose

To consider in detail the Third Person of the Trinity, the Holy Spirit, through the hymns of Charles Wesley and through scriptural accounts.

Materials

See the basic list in session 1 (p. 1).

Collect pictures and symbols that represent the Holy Spirit. Include, for example, the descending dove from the baptism of Jesus (Matthew 3:13-17; Mark 1:9-11; Luke 3:21-22), the tongues of fire (Acts 2), and the halo that surrounds the heads of persons in medieval art. Do not display these pictures immediately. If you cannot find such pictures, you may want to draw or ask someone to draw simple sketches.

Another symbol for the Holy Spirit is the breath of God, the wind of the Spirit (Genesis 2:7; Ezekiel 37:1-14). How would you picture the breath of God or the wind of the Spirit? Keep in mind that we can observe the action or effects of the wind but cannot see the wind itself. So it is with the Holy Spirit.

Prepare to Teach

At the end of the last session, you asked the group members to read chapter 4 in the study book, "The Holy Spirit" (pp. 35-44), and the section in the appendix titled "Marriage, Family, Controversy" (pp. 101-5) before this session. Be sure that you have read this material carefully.

If you have access to several hymnals, page through the sections of those hymnals devoted to the Holy Spirit. Note the number of hymns about the Holy Spirit, and compare that number with the number devoted to Jesus Christ, the Second Person of the Trinity, or to God the Creator, the First Person of the Trinity. Why do you believe most hymnals contain fewer hymns about the Holy Spirit than about the First and Second Persons of the Trinity? Why is the Holy Spirit sometimes called "the unknown person" of the Trinity?

Make copies of "Prayer to the Holy Spirit" ("Begin the Session," below) for each class member. Or you could write this prayer on a large piece of paper or on a chalkboard.

Begin the Session

Open the session with a word of welcome. Then invite the group members to pray the following prayer aloud together:

"Prayer to the Holy Spirit"

O Great Spirit,
   whose breath gives life to the world,
   and whose voice is heard in the soft breeze:
We need your strength and wisdom.
Cause us to walk in beauty. Give us eyes
   ever to behold the red and purple sunset.
Make us wise so that we may understand
   what you have taught us.
Help us learn the lessons you have hidden
   in every leaf and rock.
Make us always ready to come to you
   with clean hands and steady eyes,
so when life fades, like the fading sunset,
   our spirits may come to you without shame. Amen.
(Traditional Native American Prayer, *The United Methodist Hymnal*,
Nashville: The United Methodist Publishing House, 1989; 329)

Then, ask the group members to identify the functions of the Spirit described in the prayer.

Next, ask: What images or symbols do you associate with the Holy Spirit? As the group members provide answers, ask each to identify why a particular image or symbol represents the Holy Spirit. Urge the group members to identify biblical passages that suggest each symbol.

If group members have trouble, display the images you have brought—the dove, the tongues of fire, the halo, and so on. Talk as a whole group about why each of these images symbolizes the Holy Spirit. If time permits, speak briefly about the Spirit of God being the breath or wind of God; and ask the group members how they might symbolize this image.

Develop the Ideas

Read the words of the theme hymn, "Spirit of Faith, Come Down," antiphonally. Form two teams. Ask one team to read the first stanza aloud, then team two to read the second stanza, team one to read stanza three, and team two to read stanza four.

Have the group members, working individually, jot answers to the questions below as you read them aloud, giving them time to record their answers. The members may look at the words of the hymn as they do so.

Stanza one
1. What does the Holy Spirit reveal?
2. What does the Holy Spirit give us eyes to see?
3. Who died for every sinner?

Stanza two
4. Who is the "thou" in the third line?
5. What is the veil that needs to be taken away?

Stanza three
6. Who or what is the "all-atoning Lamb"?
7. What does the Holy Spirit demonstrate?
8. To whom does the Holy Spirit testify? What does the Holy Spirit testify?

21

Stanza four

9. How does the Holy Spirit inspire the living faith?

10. What four things does living faith do in the life of the believer?

As a whole group, go over the responses to the questions that the group members have recorded. Encourage them to respond in their own words, not simply by parroting the words of the hymn. Do all agree on the responses taken from the hymn? Why or why not? What questions do group members have about the words of the Charles Wesley hymn?

Refer to the section of the study book titled "Breathing New Life" (pp. 38-40). Call attention to the fifth full paragraph (beginning "Charles Wesley's hymns often speak of feeling God's presence and salvation.") Work in teams of three or four persons each to respond to the following questions:

How is true religion a matter of the heart as well as of the mind?

If "the heart" refers to feelings and experiences, how do we know we can trust those feelings and experiences?

Let those who will share their experiences of the Holy Spirit and how they knew that it was the Holy Spirit they were experiencing.

The Wesley hymn quoted on page 40 states, "What we have felt and seen." In what ways is "seeing" the confirmation of what we have felt, and in what ways is what we have felt the confirmation of what we have seen?

Is "seeing" always with the eyes?

How do you think Charles Wesley would answer that question?

Let those who will do so describe their experiences of "feeling his blood applied." Remember that Wesley was speaking metaphorically here. "Feeling the blood applied" represents feeling forgiven, renewed, and made one with God through the grace of Jesus Christ. It also represents the genuine humility one feels when he or she realizes the price Christ Jesus paid for her or his redemption.

Hear reports from some of the teams. If some group members would like to share their experiences of the Holy Spirit, encourage them to do so; but remind the group members that these experiences are to be shared without critique or discussion.

Wesley's hymn to the Holy Spirit speaks of a universal understanding of grace; that is, all creation will be redeemed. Wesley's hymn also speaks of "the all-atoning Lamb"; our study book writer argues that this means that "no sin is excluded from the atoning death of Jesus."

Draw a circle on the chalkboard or a large piece of paper. Label the circle "Universal Grace." Ask this question: Who or what is outside this circle of God's universal grace? Push a bit on the "what" of that question. Then, invite the group members to look up and read silently Romans 8:19-22. Raise these questions: What is the meaning of the redemption of "all creation"? What is to be redeemed in addition to persons? What part, if any, do we as human beings play in the redemption of all creation? What part does the Holy Spirit play in the redemption of all creation?

Next, ask these questions: What is the "unforgivable sin"? What sinner cannot be redeemed? Who or what sin lies outside the circle of God's grace? Expect some members to refer to Matthew 12:31-32, Mark 3:28-29, and Luke 11:10. You might want to read one or more of these passages aloud and to allow the group members to struggle with what these passages mean. Ask: How do you think Charles Wesley would respond to these questions? How did he respond to them in his hymn to the Holy Spirit that serves as the theme hymn of this chapter?

As a review of what the group has discussed about the Holy Spirit, jot on the chalkboard or a large piece of paper the main incidents from Charles Wesley's life described in the section of the appendix titled "Marriage, Family, Controversy." Discuss as a whole group: How did Wesley's understanding of the Holy Spirit, and how did his personal experience of the Holy Spirit, enter into his decision to marry and start a family? his conflicts with his brother John? his grief over his children who died in infancy? his concerns about the separation of the Methodist movement from the Church of England? Although we cannot say for sure what was in Charles's mind, his hymns about the Holy Spirit give us some insight into the ways he responded to each situation.

Draw the Session to a Close

Remind the group members that many of the hymns to and about the Holy Spirit call for the coming or the presence of the Holy Spirit. The theme hymn of this session begins in this way. Yet the Holy Spirit is among us here and now; the Holy Spirit has already come. We need not plead for the arrival of the Holy Spirit. Raise this question: If the Holy Spirit is among us, as Jesus promised, then for what should we pray regarding the Holy Spirit? Jot responses on the chalkboard or a large piece of paper, and discuss them briefly. Then invite the group members to write one-sentence prayers to or about the Holy Spirit. Ask those who will to read their prayers aloud.

Invite the group members to read chapter 5 of the study book, "The Christian Life" (pp. 45-54), and the section of the appendix titled "Closing Years" (pp. 105-7) prior to your next session. Then sing "Spirit of Faith, Come Down." Use the compact disc for accompaniment, or invite one of your group members to play the piano for the singing of the hymn.

Close with this prayer:

Holy Spirit, you are among us and within us. You are so much a part of ourselves that we are often blind and deaf to you. Awaken in us an awareness of your guiding and directing power, of your sustaining and comforting presence, of your convicting and consoling peace. Help each of us live in the surety that we do not live alone, but that you are with us every moment of our being. We pray this in the name of the Triune God. Amen.

Optional Method

Build this session "in reverse." That is, instead of focusing on the hymn text of Charles Wesley that extols the Holy Spirit, focus on the section of the appendix assigned for this session.

Using the timeline that you have developed throughout this study, add the salient incidents from Wesley's life that are described in "Marriage, Family, Controversy."

For each of these incidents, explore the presence—or the apparent absence—of the Holy Spirit as a force in Wesley's life. For example, how did the Holy Spirit enter into Charles's decision to marry Sally? In what way might the Holy Spirit have been present for both Charles and Sally during Charles's lengthy absences? What was the role of the Holy Spirit as Charles and Sally faced the deaths of some of their children?

How was the Holy Spirit present—or absent—in Charles's obvious anger with his brother John? How was the Holy Spirit present—or absent—in the theological conflicts in which Charles engaged, especially the questions of separating from the Church of England and ordaining ministers?

As the group members discuss these questions, help them comprehend, as Charles's hymn to the Holy Spirit indicates, that although the Holy Spirit is "the divine presence in our lives," none of us heeds the direction and counsel of the Holy Spirit in all of our affairs. Yet the Holy Spirit remains part of who each of us is. That is God's grace in action.

Session 5

The Christian Life

Purpose

To explore the nature of the Christian life as described in some of Charles Wesley's hymns and as reflected in incidents from his life.

Materials

See the basic list in session 1 (p. 1). Are you adding regularly to the timeline of the life of Charles Wesley?

Be sure that group members have access to Bibles, preferably in several different translations. Use translations such as the New International Version, the Contemporary English Version, Today's English Version, the New Revised Standard Version, The New English Bible, and the King James Version, to name a few. Do not use paraphrases, such as The Living Bible, unless you also use a number of good translations. Keep in mind that, writing in the eighteenth century, Charles Wesley used the King James Version; several of his hymns quote directly from the text of this version.

Prepare to Teach

Group members have been asked to read chapter 5 of the study book, "The Christian Life" (pp. 45-54), and the section of the appendix titled "Closing Years" (pp. 105-7) prior to this session. By now you should know if the group members will complete their reading prior to the sessions or if some time should be allotted during the sessions for reading the assigned chapter and other materials. Although not all of the learning activities depend on the group members' knowledge of the study book, reading the chapters in advance will equip them for richer discussion.

If you have access to a number of hymnals or sources about hymnals, look up Charles Wesley's hymn, "Come, O Thou Traveler Unknown." Sometimes this hymn is listed under the title "Wrestling Jacob." Charles Wesley wrote fourteen stanzas for this hymn, although many hymnals use only four. If you can locate all fourteen stanzas, your understanding and your group's understanding of this hymn will be enriched. Dr. Isaac Watts (1674–1748), another prolific hymn writer, was reported by John Wesley to have said, "That single poem, Wrestling Jacob, was worth all the verses he himself had written" (*The United Methodist Hymnal* [Nashville: The United Methodist Publishing House, 1989], number 387).

Begin the Session

Open this session with a word of welcome. Then offer a prayer for the group as it continues its journey of learning together. If your group has only a few members, pray for each group member by name. One of the most loving things we can do is pray aloud for one another by name.

Then, ask this question: How many different ways do you use the word *love*? Ask for examples of how this word is used in different contexts, such as (to name a few) "I love ice cream," "I love the New York Yankees," "I love Rachmaninoff's Second Piano Concerto," "I love my dog," "I love going to the beach," "I love my spouse," "I love the quiet after a summer rain shower," and "I love Jesus Christ." Given these various uses of the word *love*, what do the group members conclude the word means? Why has this word come to have so many meanings? What might happen to the core meaning of a word if it is used in so many different ways?

If time permits, you might remind the group members that several different Greek words used in the New Testament are translated by our single English word *love*. One Greek word means the physical attraction that exists between a woman and a man; another word suggests the love siblings have for one another or that good friends share; yet another word, the familiar *agape,* relates to the special kind of love God has for us. Then, ask: What makes the love God has for us different from any other kind of love? How is God's love for us similar to other kinds of love?

Develop the Ideas

Ask four members of your group to read aloud the four stanzas of "Love Divine, All Loves Excelling" (pp. 45-46 in the study book). Encourage these readers to pause fully at the periods, the exclamation points, and even at the semicolons. This hymn may be so familiar to group members that some miss the words. Caution: Reading hymns, especially hymns that rhyme, without focusing on the rhythmic pattern is difficult. Assign the four readers in advance, and encourage them to practice reading the words of this hymn as prose, not poetry.

After the group members have heard the reading of the text of this theme hymn, ask: To whom is this hymn addressed? Is this a hymn about God or Christ? Or is it about the Holy Spirit? Might the hymn be about the Trinity, God the Three in One? Where do you see the creator God in this hymn? In what ways does this hymn extol the savior Son? How is the Holy Spirit recognized in this hymn? Or is this hymn basically a prayer to God? How often does the word *love* (or a form of the word *love*) occur in these four stanzas? Does the word *love* in this hymn have the same meaning each time it is used (regardless of the form in which it is used), or is the word used in several different ways (as the opening activity demonstrated that the word is used in many different ways in our common speech)? Encourage the group members to support their responses with lines from Wesley's hymn.

Next, invite the group members to talk in pairs about possible responses to these questions: Is love a feeling, an attitude, a lifestyle, or what? How is love portrayed in this hymn of Charles Wesley? What lines from the hymn speak of love as a feeling or emotion? What lines speak of love as an action, as doing something? Does Charles Wesley describe love in this hymn more often as feeling or as doing? What, then, might you conclude about the nature of the love

Wesley is describing? How do you think the experiences that Charles Wesley had throughout his lifetime influenced his understanding of both human and divine love?

After an appropriate length of time, ask several pairs to comment on the conversation they had. Did most of the pairs reach the same conclusions? In what ways is God's love an active, doing, involved love? What has God done to demonstrate God's love for us?

The study book writer emphasizes that the Wesleys were vitally concerned with the least, the last, and the lost of their day. Although raised in relative luxury, both Charles and John lavished attention on the poor and visited in the prisons when inmates were considered the lowest of the low. Furthermore, the Wesleys taught that those who are committed to Christ—that is, those who possess the "love divine"—should do exactly the same.

Form three teams, and assign one of these biblical passages to each team: Matthew 25:31-46; 1 Corinthians 13; or 1 John 4:7-12. Direct each team to list the manifestations or indications of love described in the passage. Teams should also answer these questions about their passage: On whom is love lavished in this passage? What is the result of loving those on whom love is expended?

After an appropriate length of time, hear brief reports from each team. What can the group members conclude about love as blessing God and as prayer and praise (third stanza) from these passages?

Then, ask the group members to look up John 13. Ask one person to review quickly what takes place in this passage. Then, have someone read aloud John 13:34. Ask: If we are to love one another as Christ loved us, how are we to love? Help the group members recognize that Jesus' commandment is that we love as he loved. Note that he uttered this commandment after washing the feet of the disciples. Thus, if we are to love as Jesus loved, we will love in and through humbly serving one another. We will love through simple acts of kindness, empathy, and compassion. (If time permits, you might remind the group members that the love Jesus expended on the disciples through the washing of their feet was expended even on Judas, who betrayed Jesus. Thus, loving one another means humbly serving even those who are our enemies, our foes, our competition. Ask the group members why this is difficult to do.)

Wesley's hymn prayer asks that God finish God's new creation in and through us. Remind the group members that this is the meaning of John Wesley's concept of going on to perfection. It is the reflection of sanctifying grace, that grace of God that enables us to grow more Christlike every day.

As a whole group, quickly review the section of the appendix titled "Closing Years" (pp. 105-7). Complete the timeline of Charles Wesley's life. Then, review his life and ministry with questions such as these: How did Charles's early life affect his understanding of God's love? In what ways was the Holy Club experience formative for Charles? How did the hardships and disappointments endured by Charles help shape his hymns? What sustained Charles during his final years? How can contemporary Christians claim that same sustenance?

Draw the Session to a Close

Remind the group members that the title of the chapter you have been considering is "The Christian Life." Yet the chapter says little about rules and regulations for living a Christian life. Ask why this is so. Help the group members understand that the Christian life is a lifestyle of love in every situation. The only rule or commandment is to love one another. If this is obeyed sincerely, all the other so-called rules and regulations will care for themselves.

Then ask the group members to read chapter 6 of the study book, "Christian Community: The Church" (pp. 55-63), before the next session.

The theme hymn of chapter 5, "Love Divine, All Loves Excelling," is so powerful, your group will want to sing it aloud in its entirety. If your group enjoys singing, invite them to sing the words of this hymn to the tunes BEECHER and/or HYFRYDOL found on the accompanying compact disc. The words may also be sung to the tunes of the hymns "What a Friend We Have in Jesus" or "Joyful, Joyful, We Adore Thee." Sometimes, singing words to a different tune enables us to recognize new meanings in those words.

Close with this prayer:

Gracious God, whose very being manifests a love that is beyond our comprehension: We seek to live out your perfect love for us in love for one another, imperfect as our love may be. Forgive us for limiting our love to those like us. Instead, give us a new sense of mission to reach out to the forgotten, the neglected, and the ostracized, and to love them as Christ loved us when we had separated ourselves from him by our sinfulness. Lord Christ, give feet and hands and heart and soul to the love we seek to spend in your name. Amen.

Optional Method

If your group enjoys in-depth Bible study and has basic Bible study skills, try this: Distribute concordances (these need not be exhaustive concordances); and invite the group members, working in teams, to look up scriptural passages that contain the word *love*. For the purposes of this exercise, limit this search to the New Testament. Ask the teams to consider these kinds of questions: How is the word *love* used most often in the New Testament? Is the word *love* used consistently, that is, with the same meaning, throughout the New Testament? Illustrate your response. In most examples from the New Testament, who is doing the loving and who is being loved?

Hear brief reports from each team, then examine Charles Wesley's hymn "Love Divine, All Loves Excelling." How does Wesley use the word *love* in this hymn? What is the scriptural basis for his characterization of love in this hymn?

Using chapter 5 and the appendix of the study book, invite the group members to consider these questions: What was Charles Wesley's understanding of love as reflected in his hymns? How might Charles Wesley have come to this understanding of love? How was Charles Wesley's understanding of love reflected in his life? Push for specifics at this point. Then ask this question: Do you think loving as Wesley described it is easier for us than it was for him? Why or why not?

Session 6

Christian Community:
The Church

Purpose

To deepen and enrich an understanding of the church as God's creation by looking at some of the hymn texts of Charles Wesley.

Materials

See the basic list in session 1 (p. 1).

Although the focus of these sessions is on the texts or the words of some of Charles Wesley's hymns, include the singing of the hymns in your sessions. The compact disc included in this leader's guide provides the music or accompaniment for the theme hymns, including alternative tunes for some of the hymns. If you have access to a piano and a competent pianist, you may want to invite the group to sing the hymns to additional alternative tunes. The use of the metrical index in the back of most hymnals will help you locate such tunes. Bear in mind that Charles Wesley did not write many melodies for his hymns; he borrowed tunes, or others set his poetry to music. Therefore, singing his hymns to tunes other than the familiar ones does not do injustice to Charles Wesley.

Prepare to Teach

Group members were asked to read chapter 6, "Christian Community: The Church" (pp. 55-63), of the study book, prior to this session. If the majority of the group members have not read this chapter, you may need to allow time for them to read portions of the chapter during the session.

Charles Wesley was a member of the clergy of the Church of England and as such held to those confessions of faith of the Church of England that described the nature of the church. As the Methodist movement grew and expanded, this growth demonstrated that Methodism was not just a reform movement within the Church of England, as the Wesleys intended from the beginning, but was indeed becoming a denomination on its own. Charles Wesley's brother John forwarded to the Methodist societies in North America a series of faith statements, based in part on the confessions of the Church of England, to which he invited the North American Methodists to adhere. Although Charles Wesley's involvement in preparing these statements is not clear, John's habit of checking almost everything with Charles and with others would suggest that Charles knew of and supported these statements.

The Wesley statement about the church is simple and clear: "The visible Church of Christ is a congregation of faithful men in which the pure Word of God is preached, and the Sacraments duly administered according to Christ's ordinance, in all those things that of necessity are requisite to the same" (*The Book of Discipline of The United Methodist Church* [Nashville: The United Methodist Publishing House, 2000], 62). Wesley's use of the word *men* reflects the time in which he wrote (1784). Both Wesleys included women in prominent positions in the movement from the very beginning, perhaps as a result of the strong influence that their mother, Susanna Wesley, had upon them.

Note too the practical nature of Wesley's statement. He did not define so much what the church *is* as describe what the church *does*. You and your group will see this clearly in Charles Wesley's hymns about the church.

Begin the Session

Open this session with a greeting. Then, invite the group members to bow in prayer. Ask each to pray in silence for the church, the community of believers, gathered in this place. Then ask each to pray in silence for the Church universal, the gathering of Christ's people whomever and wherever they might be. Close this time of prayer with a brief prayer praising God for the creation of the church and affirming the commitment of the group to Christ's church, Christ's presence, in the world.

Ask each group member to write a one-sentence definition of what the church *is* or what the church *does*. You might use a simple sentence stem to begin: *The church is . . .* or *The church does. . . .* Also ask the group members to refrain from referring to the study book as they write their sentences.

Form teams of three persons each, and let each person share her or his definition with the other members of the team. After an appropriate length of time, hear some of the definitions in the whole group. Are most of the definitions descriptions of what the church *is* or descriptions of what the church *does*? Why do you think this is so?

Then ask: What did the Wesleys believe about the church as the body of Christ? Allow time for a brief discussion, then share with the group the statement written by John Wesley for the Methodist movement in North America, quoted above. Note the practical nature of this definition.

(If time permits, you might point out that John Wesley, the older brother of Charles, was a priest of the Church of England and continued in that capacity until his death. It was not John's wish to begin a new denomination. He was interested in reforming and bringing new life to the Church of England. The Methodist movement outgrew both Wesleys, however, and became the several denominations we now know as the Wesleyan and Methodist groups of churches.)

Develop the Ideas

The theme hymn of this chapter, "Christ, From Whom All Blessings Flow," may not be as well known to your group members as the other hymns you have been studying. This may work to your advantage as some group members may be hearing these words for the first time. You might sing this hymn as a group before beginning your discussions. Use the compact disc that accompanies this leader's guide to provide the tune.

Next, ask six group members to read the stanzas of the hymn aloud. Have two persons read aloud together stanzas one and four, two other persons read aloud together stanzas two and five, and the other two persons read stanzas three and six. If possible, invite these three teams of readers to stand in different areas of your meeting space, such as a team on each side of the meeting area and a team in the back of the meeting space. As these stanzas are read aloud, invite the group members to follow along in their study books and to jot down any ideas or insights they gain about the nature of the church, the Christian community, from the words of this hymn.

Form six teams (a team can be as few as one person; if your group is small in number, assign two sets of questions to a team). Ask each team to focus on one of the six stanzas of the theme hymn. Using both the hymn text and the comments made by the study book writer, ask the teams to consider responses to these questions (you may want copy these questions in advance to give to the teams):

Stanza one

Who are the "saints" and what makes them "saintly"? Are saints only those who have died? Is one "once a saint, always a saint"? Give reasons for your answer.

Why does Charles Wesley refer to the church as the "mystic body"? What is mysterious about the church as you know it and experience it? as it should be ideally? In what ways does the church exemplify the cliché, "The whole is greater than the sum of its parts"?

Stanza two

How would you rephrase or summarize the point of this stanza? Write a paraphrase of this stanza. Be ready to share this paraphrase with the whole group.

Stanza three

What is the common work we are called to fulfill? Can you state this in one simple sentence? What are some of the diverse gifts Christ provides us to fulfill that work? Be specific in naming or listing these gifts.

Stanza four

What is the grace that is bestowed on each member of the Christian community?

What is the meaning of the phrase "tempered by the art of God"? How does God temper us? (Think here of "tempering" a fine piece of steel so that it can hold an edge.) If *tempered* is a difficult word to use here, think of some synonyms. What word would you use in place of "tempered"?

Stanza five

This stanza calls us all one in Christ. How do you experience that oneness in your congregation? How can you experience that oneness in the worldwide church? How can you experience oneness with Christians in China, in Africa, in Iraq, and set in South America—as well as with Christians of various denominations in North America? What is the nature of that oneness?

Stanza six

Give special attention to the study book writer's discussion of the similarities between love and death (pp. 61-63). If these are the great levelers of all humankind, how can we build upon the leveling quality of love to ensure unity in our congregations, in our communities, and in our world? Is it Christ's intention that this leveling takes place? What does leveling mean in this instance?

After an appropriate length of time, hear a brief report from each of the six teams. Encourage the teams not simply to read the questions they were asked and the answers they provided, but also to describe how their stanzas and the insights they gained from those stanzas define and describe the church as it should be.

Next, stage a mock debate. Invite four volunteers to form two debating teams. Ask two persons to be a team that will support the argument, "We must all be exactly alike if we are to be the church." Ask the other two persons to be the team that will take the opposite side: "We must all be different and have different gifts if we are to be the church."

Give the two debating teams a few minutes to prepare their opening statements. Let each team make a one-minute opening statement, then each team has one minute to rebut the opening statement made by the other team. Then let each team have a one minute closing statement. (Expect some laughter here; you may be asking persons to support positions they do not hold themselves.)

Allow some comments from the "audience" of the debate, then call the attention of the group to the four reasons why God gives us differing gifts, found in the study book (p. 59). Go over these reasons briefly. Then, ask the group members to bow and thank God in silence for the unique gifts they have received.

Draw the Session to a Close

Reread the Wesleys' definition of the church (see "Prepare to Teach," above). Then, raise this question for brief discussion: How does the theme hymn for this chapter and the Wesleys' statement on the church help you understand what the church is and must be? Is the church today fulfilling that description? Why or why not?

Sing the theme hymn together again, using the compact disc for accompaniment. Or select a more familiar tune from the metrical index in your hymnal.

Ask the group members to read chapter 7, "The Lord's Supper" (pp. 65-73 of the study book), before your group meets again.

Close by asking the group members to pray silently; then offer this prayer:

Lord Christ, you have created the church to be your abiding presence on earth until your coming again. Strengthen and purify your church so that we who claim to be the church can truly glorify your name and implement your holy will. We pray for our congregation of your church and we pray for congregations in all places as together we seek to lift your name. It is in that name that we pray. Amen.

Optional Method

The questions at the conclusion of the appendix in the study book (p. 63) are particularly precise and thought provoking. You might choose to concentrate on discussing responses to these six questions as a whole group. Or, if your group enjoys working in small teams, assign one of the questions to each of six teams, give the teams several minutes to discuss their question, and then hear reports from each of the teams. Make this reporting time a time of genuine discussion, not simply hearing what a team representative says. Be sure to monitor the time carefully so that each team can make its report.

Session 7

The Lord's Supper

Purpose

To enrich and deepen an understanding of the Sacrament of the Lord's Supper through a consideration of several of Charles Wesley's hymns on this subject.

Materials

See the basic list in session 1 (p. 1).

Collect objects and illustrations symbolizing the Sacrament of the Lord's Supper. These might include a chalice (a large cup) and paten (the plate on which the communion bread is placed), individual communion cups, visual depictions or symbols of the bread and grapes, a loaf of unsliced bread, communion wafers (round coin-shaped wafers or small square wafers), and so forth. Place these objects and illustrations around your meeting room before the group members arrive.

If you choose to celebrate the Sacrament of the Lord's Supper as part of this session, prepare a worship center on which to place the bread and cup. You may want to put a small cross and candlesticks (if available) on the table. Check with your pastor about the type of bread she or he wishes to use and whether he or she wishes to use a common cup (the chalice) or individual communion cups.

Prepare to Teach

Copy on a large piece of paper or chalkboard John Wesley's statement on the nature of the Sacrament of the Lord's Supper (p. 66 in the study book).

If you are considering sharing in the Sacrament of the Lord's Supper during this session, talk at length with your pastor before doing so. Denominational rules and customs vary widely. In some denominations, only ordained pastors can consecrate the communion elements; in other denominations, any believing Christian can conduct the Sacrament of the Lord's Supper. A word of caution: You may think you know the traditions and requirements in your denomination, but you *must* talk with your pastor to verify your understanding and to ensure that the tradition of your denomination is carried out with integrity.

Additionally, determine where the Sacrament of Holy Communion will be conducted. In some situations, the sacrament can be observed in your meeting room; in others, you may want to move to a chapel or to your church's sanctuary or nave to conduct the service. Again, a conversation with your pastor is crucial at this point.

Your group may want to sing the theme hymn for this chapter at some point during the session. As this may be an unfamiliar hymn to some members of your group, you may want to use the more familiar alternative tune on the compact disc contained in this leader's guide as the accompaniment.

Steep yourself in the theology of the Sacrament of the Lord's Supper. One of the best ways to do this is through a conversation with your pastor. You might share with your pastor the major points of chapter 7 of the study book, especially the three reasons why Holy Communion is invaluable to Christians. Does your pastor agree with these reasons? Would she or he suggest additional reasons why this Sacrament is so important? You might also ask your pastor to help you with potentially complex and controversial words and terms related to Holy Communion, such as *transubstantiation, consubstantiation,* and *real presence.*

Begin the Session

Open this session with a word of welcome. Are you checking on those whose attendance has been irregular, especially if some have been ill, traveling, or caught up in other responsibilities? Are you praying during these moments for concerns within the group? Offer a prayer that the hearts and minds of all group members will be open to the presence of the Holy Spirit in the midst of the group as you discuss the Sacrament of the Lord's Supper.

Form pairs in the group. Caution! Do not let the same two persons form a pair each time you call for pairs. Also, try to avoid having husbands and wives talk with each other when you break into pairs.

Tell the group that you are going to read several questions aloud and that individual responses to these questions are to be discussed in the pairs. Here are the questions:

- What do you feel when you participate in the Sacrament of the Lord's Supper? Push hard here for feelings, not thoughts or ideas. What is going on inside, what sensations or internal feelings do you have as you participate in Holy Communion?

- How have your feelings about participating in the Sacrament of the Lord's Supper changed over the years? Do you recall the first time you took part in Holy Communion? How did you feel then?

- Based on your feelings as you participate in Holy Communion and on your understanding of this sacrament, what does Holy Communion mean to you each time you participate?

- (If time permits) In some congregations, persons do not attend worship on those Sundays when they know Holy Communion will be served. Why do you think this may be so?

After an appropriate length of time, ask a few pairs for brief reports. Then, jot on the large piece of paper or chalkboard some of the feelings that persons experience as they participate in the Sacrament of the Lord's Supper. Let those who said that their feelings have changed over the years describe the differences. What occasioned these changes?

Develop the Ideas

Sing the theme hymn for this session, using the compact disc for accompaniment. Then invite four persons to read aloud the four stanzas of the theme hymn, "O, the Depth of Love Divine." Encourage them to read with attention to the punctuation rather than to the rhymes of meter. Ask the group members to listen carefully as the four stanzas are read. Then, ask them to call out any new insights they gained into the meaning of the Lord's Supper through this hymn or any questions they might have about the meaning of certain phrases within the hymn. If several persons have questions about meaning, spend a few moments as a whole group exploring possible responses to the questions raised by the group members.

Next, ask a good reader to read aloud the statement about the Sacrament of the Lord's Supper that John Wesley sent to the Methodist societies in North America (p. 66 in the study book or printed on a large piece of paper or chalkboard). Ask the group members to follow in their study books or to read the statement printed on a large piece of paper or chalkboard.

Then, ask: How does the theme hymn support Wesley's statement about the Lord's Supper? Do you see any contradictions between the theme hymn and the statement by John Wesley? If so, what?

The writer of the study book makes several salient points with regard to the Sacrament of the Lord's Supper. Deal with those points in this way:

Form three teams.

Assign one team to study and discuss carefully the section titled "Unfathomable Grace." In addition to their own questions about this section, invite them to deal with queries such as: What does the word *unfathomable* mean? What other words might you use to express this reality? How does our cognitive understanding (that is, our reason, intellect, logical comprehension) of grace interfere with our faith understanding of unfathomable grace? What part does reason play in our experience of the Sacrament of the Lord's Supper?

Team two will look at the section titled "Bread and Wine Convey God's Power" and discuss in some detail the ideas in this portion of the study book. Then consider questions such as these: Why does Wesley refer to the elements as "feeble"? What was he trying to communicate by the use of this adjective? Do the bread and wine convey God's power through the Sacrament of Holy Communion? Or does something else convey that power to us? If so, what?

Team three will read the section of the study book chapter titled "Mystery Ordained by Christ" and discuss these questions: What are the major points the study book writer is making in this section?

What does the word *mystery* mean? What does the fact that Holy Communion is a mystery mean to us? Is this a mystery to be solved? If not, then what do we do with this mystery? What does the word *ordained* mean in this section's title? Does this imply an imperative or a directive? If this is a directive, is participation in the Sacrament of the Lord's Supper necessary for salvation? Why or why not?

After an appropriate length of time, hear a quick summary report from each team. Encourage the whole group to raise questions or to make comments regarding each team's report. (If questions arise, this might be the time to discuss phrases and words, perhaps known in part to some group members, such as *transubstantiation, consubstantiation, real presence*, and so forth. Be careful not to belittle another denomination's understanding of the role of the elements in the Sacrament of Holy Communion. Recognizing differences in perception and belief can deepen and enrich our understanding of the Lord's Supper.)

Draw the Session to a Close

As a whole group, sing the theme hymn for this chapter again, using the compact disc for accompaniment. Then, ask these questions: Did you find new meaning in this hymn as we just sang it; that is, insights that you did not gain when we sang it at the opening of the session? If so, what? What have you learned about Holy Communion as a result of this session's discussions?

If you have made arrangements in advance with your pastor, participate in the Sacrament of the Lord's Supper, using the ritual of your denomination. When the time for the sharing of the bread arrives, discuss the different forms the bread may take (loaf, wafers, and so forth), emphasizing that all are symbols of Christ's presence. So too with the cup. Discuss the various forms of sharing the cup, such as the common cup, intinction (dipping a piece of bread into the cup), or distributing individual cups. Emphasize that all forms are equally valid; the meaning of the act is far more important than the externals of the act.

After all have partaken of the Lord's Supper and the ritual is completed, ask the group members to form pairs to discuss any feelings or insights each person may have had as she or he participated in this sacrament. Do not be afraid to focus on feelings rather than on thoughts. What happens to us as we partake of the bread and the cup in response to Jesus' injunction: "Do this, as often as you eat and drink it, in remembrance of me"?

After an appropriate length of time, ask the group members to read chapter 8 in the study book, "Christ's Resurrection and Christian Hope" (pp. 75-84), prior to your next session.

End this session by inviting the group to read slowly and in unison the three stanzas of the Charles Wesley poem that concludes chapter 7 in the study book (p. 73).

Optional Method

Many denominations use a specified liturgy when celebrating the Sacrament of the Lord's Supper. A liturgy is the body of words and actions used in public worship. In many cases, some elements of the liturgy always remain the same, while other elements vary with the season of the year or special occasions. Some denominations use extensive liturgies for celebrating the Lord's Supper; others use brief liturgies. In each case, the liturgies, both in word and in action, are filled with meaning.

Lead your group in a careful, step-by-step study of the Communion liturgy used in your denomination. You may want to invite your pastor to assist you, to make comments and answer questions. Or, you may need to borrow resources from your pastor in order to go through the liturgy in detail.

As you go through the liturgy, keep questions such as these in mind: What do the words convey? What meanings are inherent in the actions of the liturgy (such as the breaking of the bread or the celebrant's [pastor's] position as the liturgy is being conducted)? How do the words and the actions of the liturgy used for the Sacrament of the Lord's Supper in your denomination coincide with the major points of the theme hymn of this chapter and with the other Wesleyan hymns mentioned in this chapter?

Session 8

Christ's Resurrection and Christian Hope

Purpose

To consider in some detail the affirmations about death and life everlasting declared in Charles Wesley's Easter hymn.

Materials

See the basic list in session 1 (p. 1).

Did your study group complete the timeline of Charles Wesley's life? If so, you may want to reproduce the timeline in hand-out form for the members of your group.

Examine the excellent bibliography the writer of the study book provides following the appendix (pp. 109-10). Collect as many of these books as you can. Perhaps your pastor will have some of the titles or know where copies may be borrowed. Check your local library, and provide the group members with a list of the books that are available. The purpose of gathering these books is to encourage and enable group members to continue their study of Charles Wesley and his hymns with the goal of understanding the Christian faith more completely.

Prepare to Teach

If time permits, scan some of the collected books on Charles and John Wesley and on the early history of the Methodist and Wesleyan movement. Examine the tables of contents and browse through chapters that catch your attention. Be ready and prepared to recommend two or three of the books to group members who may want to continue their study of the Christian faith through hymnody.

Have you been using the compact disc in this leader's guide to accompany the Wesleyan hymns used in this study? If so, set up your compact disc player to play the theme hymn for today, "Christ the Lord Is Risen Today," as group members gather for the session.

Go through this session plan carefully and be comfortable in your own understanding of the resurrection of Jesus Christ.

You may want to prepare worksheets for the questions about the six stanzas of the theme hymn. Do this by jotting the questions for each team on a piece of paper, leaving plenty of room for responses.

The study book writer points out that the crucifixion of Jesus Christ is central to some Christian denominations; indeed, some denominations adorn their places of worship with pictures, statues, or symbols of Jesus Christ on the cross. Historically, this is an emphasis of what is known as "Western Christianity," or that Christianity that developed in Rome and spread into Europe. "Eastern Christianity," or the Christianity that developed in Greek-speaking regions and spread eastward (present in what we now know as the Greek Orthodox and other Orthodox churches), focuses somewhat less on the Crucifixion and somewhat more on the Resurrection. Both Eastern and Western Christianity are, of course, correct. As the study book writer indicates, the Crucifixion was necessary for the Resurrection to take place; but without the Resurrection, the Crucifixion would simply have been the martyrdom of a good man.

Although Charles Wesley wrote his resurrection hymn as an Easter hymn, we can assume that he hoped that it would be used more than one Sunday each year.

Begin the Session

Open the session by inviting the group members to sing "Christ the Lord Is Risen Today" as triumphantly as possible. Use the compact disc accompaniment; this will ensure that the singing does not drag but remains triumphant.

As this is probably your last session, pray for each group member by name if your group is small. You should know each group member well enough to make your words personal.

Then, ask each group member to turn to one other group member and to answer this question: What does the resurrection of Jesus Christ mean to you?

Develop the Ideas

Before discussing Charles Wesley's Easter hymn, spend a few moments as a whole group talking about the difference between "resurrection" and "resuscitation." You might do this by asking for similarities and differences between Lazarus, Jairus's daughter, and the widow's son at Nain "coming back to life" and the resurrection of Jesus. Help the group members understand that the first three were resuscitated, that is, returned to the life they had had. Jesus was resurrected, that is, given a *new* life, a new beginning. This is why Mary did not immediately recognize him in the garden (John 20) and why the disciples did not know him on the road to Emmaus (Luke 24). Resurrection is not being brought back to one's former life, but instead being given a new life, perhaps in a new form. (Some group members may point out quite accurately that Lazarus and the others died again; Jesus as the resurrected one lives eternally.)

Next, ask six persons each to read aloud one of the stanzas of the theme hymn. Direct the readers to leave out the "alleluias." This is so the whole group can hear and focus on the direct message Charles Wesley was communicating.

For many persons, this hymn is so familiar that the subtleties of its message may be overlooked or lost. In order to counteract this possibility, try this approach.

Form six teams (recall that a team can be as few as one person; if you have fewer than six persons, assign two or more stanzas to each person). Ask each team to focus on one of the stanzas of the Wesley hymn and to think about the following questions concerning their stanza. (If you jotted these questions on worksheets beforehand, distribute them now.)

Stanza one

What is implied in Wesley's two phrases, "Earth and heaven in chorus say," and "Sing, ye heavens, and earth reply"? Christ is Lord of whom and of what? Refer to Romans 8:31-39.

Stanza two

What is the fight, the battle that was won? Is death the foe? If so, from where did death come? Did God create death as part of life? If God created all things, did God also create death? If death is not the foe in this stanza, what is the foe?

Stanzas three

What does Wesley imply when he refers to Jesus Christ as "King"? What is included in the concept of kingship that is especially appropriate for Christ Jesus? Is the sting of death overcome completely by the resurrection of Christ Jesus? If we can conclude that Wesley is not saying that the death of a loved one does not bring grief (recall Wesley's own personal grief over the loss of loved ones), then what is the "sting of death" about which he wrote?

Stanza four

Describe in some detail what Charles Wesley meant when he proclaimed that we are made like Christ Jesus and will rise like Christ Jesus. One of the most powerful affirmations in this hymn is the last line of the fourth stanza. What exactly is Wesley claiming when he proclaims—with joy—that ours, too, is the cross and the grave and finally the skies? What is our cross? our grave? For what is *skies* a metaphor in this stanza?

Stanza five

What is Wesley proclaiming when he refers to Christ as Lord of both earth and heaven? If Christ is Lord of the earth, does this include more than just the people of earth? If so, what does it mean? How do the third and fourth lines of this stanza make the point that Jesus Christ was not resuscitated, but indeed resurrected?

Stanza six

In what ways is Christ both king of glory and soul of bliss? Recall definitions of *glory* used earlier in this study. What is *bliss*? Refer to John 14:27 and Philippians 4:7. How can Jesus and Paul promise peace in the midst of imminent danger—Jesus spoke the words in John just prior to his arrest, and Paul wrote to the Philippians while he was in prison?

Allow the six teams several minutes to formulate their responses. Note that these are not "yes or no" or "factual" questions, but questions that require thought and reflection.

Hear brief reports from each of the six teams. Encourage the teams not just to read the questions and to recite their answers, but instead to discuss what is contained in their stanzas, using the questions as possible starting places.

Next, focus on the concept of Christian hope. Invite the group members to refer again to the theme hymn and to the hymn "Rejoice, the Lord Is King!" (pp. 75-76 and 80-81 of the study book). For Wesley, what was the Christian hope? The group members will probably describe Wesley's concept of Christian hope as the hope of heaven, glory with Christ. Then, ask: How did Charles Wesley describe heaven in these two hymns? If the group members have trouble answering, help them see that Wesley did not describe heaven as Revelation 21 describes heaven. Instead, Wesley gave no details other than implying fellowship with Christ as a dimension of heaven and suggesting that heaven is our eternal home. Why do the group members think Wesley avoided detailed descriptions of heaven?

Next, ask the group members, working individually, to write one-sentence definitions of Christian hope, the "Glorious Hope" Wesley declared in stanza four of "Rejoice, the Lord Is King." Before inviting several group members to read their definitions, talk about what Christian hope is not. Christian hope is not a wish list or a Christmas list; it is not a pie-in-the-sky dream; it is not wishful thinking; it is not a longing for something that seems impossible. Hear a few of the one-sentence definitions of Christian hope written by the group members. Then discuss what Christian hope is. Christian hope *is* a life lived in the assurances of the promises of God, a life lived in an abiding faith that God's promises are trustworthy and true. Invite the group to go back over the two hymns, "Christ the Lord Is Risen Today" and "Rejoice! The Lord Is King," for clear evidence of Wesley's belief in this concept of Christian hope.

Draw the Session to a Close

Sing again the theme hymn for this session. Discuss this question briefly: The word *Alleluia* means "praise Yah[weh]" or "praise God," as the study book writer declares. If we were to write this hymn in today's language, what word might we use in place of *Alleluia?* What word or phrase do we use to declare our praises to God in Christ?

If time permits, ask each group member to reflect on the past eight sessions and to write a paragraph of no more than four sentences summarizing insights gained from this study that will strengthen or illuminate her or his faith. Did the group members find more meaning in the chapters about the Trinity? about the church? about Christian living? about the resurrection hope? After an appropriate length of time, ask a few of the group members to share their paragraphs.

Close the session with this prayer:

Lord of melody and harmony, Lord of the music of the spheres, Lord of life and hope: We bow before you in humble thanksgiving and expectation, claiming the promises you have made to us and for us and living in that Christian hope that enables us to live triumphantly even in the midst of suffering, disappointment, and grief. Because you, Lord of life, know our life and share in it with us, we claim you as one with us yet infinitely beyond us. Thanks be to God. Amen.

Optional Methods

Invite the group members to recall the first time they heard the theme hymn for this session. This assumes that most are familiar with this hymn, for it is a popular Easter hymn. Then, ask the group members to recall and describe their feelings as this hymn is sung as part of a worship service at Easter and as part of a worship service at a time other than Easter.

Then, ask the group members to consider what makes this hymn such a powerful statement of the Resurrection. Is it the tune? (These words can be sung to the familiar tunes used with "Jesus, Lover of My Soul," "Come, Ye Thankful People, Come," or "Take My Life, and Let It Be.") Is it the words? Is it the combination of words and music?

Ask the group members to focus their attention on particular stanzas of the theme hymn and to select words and phrases that especially speak to them.

Then, turn to the six questions that the study book writer provides at the close of chapter 8 (pp. 83-84) and discuss these questions in teams or as a whole group.